TALKING CURE

TALKING CURE

poems by
Lisa Zeidner

Texas Tech Press
Lubbock, Texas, U.S.A.
1982

Acknowledgments

Permission from the following to reprint the poems listed is gratefully acknowledged.

Antioch Review, Vol. 35, No. 2-3 (Spring-Summer 1977), copyright 1977: "Freud Is Dead"
Black Warrior Review: "Because I Can't"
Epoch: "Directions," "The Sadness of Women"
The Little Magazine: "Light"
Mississippi Review: "Cannibals," "Diner," "An Etiquette for Automatic Writing," "God's Jukebox," "Man, Ladder, Wall, Elephant, and Fly," "Mica," "Mind the Quiet," "Teaching Him to Read," "Tornado Warning"
Selections: University & College Poetry Prizes, 1973-78, The Academy of American Poets: "Still"
Shenandoah, copyright 1978 by Washington and Lee University: "Skinner Remembers a Fall"
Three Rivers Poetry Journal, copyright 1981 by Three Rivers Press: "Bach"
West Branch: "The Madonna Has That Look Again"

Talking Cure, by Lisa Zeidner, is published in cooperation with the Associated Writing Programs and is an *AWP Award Series Selection*.

ISBN 0-89672-094-2 (paper)
ISBN 0-89672-095-0 (cloth)
Library of Congress Catalog Card Number: 81-52502
Designed by Betty M. Johnson, set in Highland,
printed on Texas Tech Opaque, 70 lb.
Cover and dust jacket design by Colette Gaiter
Texas Tech Press, Lubbock, Texas 79409
Copyright 1982 by Texas Tech University
Printed in the United States of America

Foreword

Lisa Zeidner's work is fugal—the ordinary is joined by the ordinary and strange to make the extraordinary. In "Mica," rush hour traffic noises cover the music made by the waitress playing the harp on a fire escape "so all that reaches/ you is her perfect glissando, the notes/slow and whole as figs, each note/gold as the blond hair spun on legs/you'd see better, if you moved closer." As in a fugue, the new lines enter extending the work past the natural stopping point of each phase so the poems continually re-engage; small moments become longer spans; the counterpoint delights and lifts the reader who looks back and says, how did I get here?

That question is asked not out of confusion—the sidewalk, with its intrinsic bits of mica sparkling like dissonant collisions in a fugue, does not disappear over a cliff as it would in a cartoon or in the poems of certain surrealists; it is coherent and can be walked on again—the question is asked because there is a sense in Zeidner's work that the pleasures she gives us on the journey make the difficult seem seductively easy. Imagine Bellini variations on a theme by Bach. Or as she says in "Bach," imagine the music made when "My left hand's a flying fish,/ my right hand's a swimming bird."

Of course the equation of the ordinary and extraordinary can be played the other way, too, a mirror fugue, so that the extraordinary is joined by itself to illumine the ordinary:

> It is true that each time a native dies
> these cannibals eat a tourist,
> but the rest of the time
> this tribe does lovely things with trees.
> ("Cannibals")

> Men are born with erections and die with them.
> From the first slap men stiffen and are sad.
> Erections are broomsticks which propel men
> from the womb and ride men into the world
> so they can be Bach and the hangman, crack
> the safes, make the Louisiana Purchase
> and teach the dolphins to talk.
> ("The Sadness of Men")

The themes of Zeidner's poems and those of her fine novel, *Customs*, are time; birth; death; her own generation and those before and after; sex and love; and even, unfashionably, God. What a task for a poet still in her twenties, yet her sleight of hand—the flying fish, the swimming bird, the wit, intelligence and sensuality—make her able not only to manage it but to achieve the grand and avoid the grandiose. The long poem "Make-Up" deals with the concerns of those growing up in the sixties and seventies as sadly, truly, funnily, as "A Maturation Poem" does with masturbation: "Did Helen of Troy masturbate in captivity, did Cleopatra or did she get a maidservant to do it for her, one fanning her with a feather, another tucking skinned olives into her mouth?"

As we admire light glittering off the strands of these poems, strands which mesh together to enmesh the reader, we gradually sense that the poet is afraid and alone at the center of the web she weaves to catch us. We are captured willingly, first by the pleasurable lures, then more completely, by the recognition of our shared fears so bravely addressed—"we've all tasted our own flesh"—but she is caught, too. And it is the tension between all these ensnaring elements which truly binds us to Zeidner's poems. For a time we almost forget where we are; the flights of her strong imagination cause us to enter that other kind of fugue from which we escape knowing we are changed but not quite understanding how, carried along by "her perfect glissando."

Cynthia Macdonald
Houston, Texas
November 1981

Contents

One morning after a pleasant fall of snow I sent a letter to someone with whom I had business, but failed to mention the snow. The reply was amusing: "Do you suppose that I shall take any notice of what someone says who is so perverse that he writes a letter without a word of inquiry about how I am enjoying the snow? I am most disappointed in you." Now that the author of that letter is dead, even so trivial an incident sticks in my mind.

—The Tsurezuregusa of Kenko,
Essays in Idleness

For Laura Walworth

I

Mica

Behind laundry on the fire escape
a waitress you recognize plays the harp.
The clothes shift: you can just make out
the lazy curve of her knee, and if
there are wrong notes they're veiled

by rush hour, so all that reaches
you is her perfect glissando, the notes
slow and whole as figs, each note
gold as the blond hair spun on legs
you'd see better, if you moved closer—

but then you'd have to speak to her,
and what would you say? That you love her
so much each bit of mica embedded
in pavement moves you? If so,
why didn't you mention this earlier,

when you watched her pal around
with the slow-witted busboy? You might
have offered to take her coral-reefing:
imagine her with a garland of minnows,
playing the harp underwater, and you!—

tanned, intelligent, informed about wines,
telling her how the Chinese sold unicorn's
horns as the West sold pieces of the cross;
how thousands of Swiss children in berets
spend every June harvesting one basket

of microscopic flowers that make one
ounce of perfume for one rich woman—
but that would be another, more photogenic
kind of love. That would be fool's gold.
You loved her quite enough

on the fire escape you've already passed,
and when you get home—even if there isn't
mail—you'll put on Bach, sit by fruit
almost ripe on the table and be,
for her, exceedingly quiet.

Still

We still want to say the one true thing
we almost said by that pond in the beginning.

One of us skipped a rock instead, not well,
and offered something parodoxical:

Then we wanted now. Then, we said, will be best.
Though we know better now, we still miss then.

Later, snowed in—though the only elements
were typographical—we read *Hamlet*

out loud, watching words clink through ice.
How distinct a word was then, how crisp!

What is this homesickness?
What do we think we've lost?

Though nothing's wrong, we still suspect
the true thing must be said in verse—so what,

we therefore ask, is verse? The reverse
of how we've spoken all these years?

If so, when did we grow prosaic? Why?
I tell you everything we did was poetry:

our words were stepping stones across
the fairy tale pond, meandering and mossy,

yet getting us somewhere—here, perhaps.
Of course it's more complicated than that.

You reminded me—we had a history even then—
how I once said, *You are the perfect sentence.*

I remembered a scarf of yours, bright red.
Was that the true thing needing to be said?

Let's say it to this vulnerable snow, tonight.
This snow, unsaying itself on the pavement.

Light

My mother left three fingers of light
between me and outside
when she closed my door at bedtime,

because the man with a thousand eyes
could walk in if my door were open
and kick in my door if it were closed,

but if it were ajar he got confused
and had to enter some other child's nightmare.
He was scared of half-light; me, of half-life.

I was too young to die.
I thought the dust was cancer: it flew
in a laser from the blinds, lighter

than light, right towards my bed—I pulled
the heavy blanket over my head and hoped
that cancer would overlook me as God had.

I couldn't breathe. It was like death alone
under that blanket; it wasn't funny.
Downstairs, I could make out the charms

light as laughter on all the wrists
of all my mother's fat friends,
the deadly hum of their fluorescents—

"Edith's going in for chemotherapy."
The fat guests made our house bottom-heavy.
My bedroom was going to float away

too close to the sun and melt, I'd never
be called inside for dinner again,
I didn't want to stay awake forever

weightless in space in my blue feet pajamas
like a moonsuit—and it was dark in space too.
Space was one big grave, and it wanted me.

I stood by the bannister overlooking their party.
It was so light down there, so cool,
their drinks clear as water but different, safer.

A Morse code of weightless blue pajama-fluff
alit on them then, like messages from space.
There was only one note in my spectrum—it meant

Me. Me. Me.

The Birth of Words

Let's say Earth was a good-natured whore God sometimes deigned to make love to. But since there was no language, and since God had no form, He couldn't have courted Earth with a mime and a bunch of daisies. Still, if we try to imagine their lovemaking as the ancients imagined it—as a barometric condition, Homer's rosy-fingered dawn a rash on Earth's chest—we find we can't avoid, say, His tongue in her ear. His "hands." So while we can construct a story about a grain of sand lodged in Earth's channel that, christened by their lovemaking and flung on the beach, begins to permute into a chorus of sounds, making wild leaps and transgressions until a language is born, we find we cannot avoid using the anachronistic word *christened*. And while it is tempting (a low rumble of *smorgasbord* and *wanderlust* rising from the waterline), we cannot have God sit like the Divine Child constructing galaxies in the shape of words. He cannot make a fish that struggles the wrong way in its stream like the awkward consonants in the word *salmon*, nor can He be unable to think of a fish for the word *perplex* and make it, instead, the animal of uncertainty. He cannot, you see, say anything. So we're back where we started, asking why we are doing this in the first place, what the first place *is* and why we are so anxious to get there. What's wrong with the shine on our boots, our blushes made for love?

And dinner's on; I'm chopping onions. My wrist is swift and final. It seems to say: *Chicken and egg. Chicken and egg.* The tears on my face are not real. You say you love my eyes and I say *Yes. I remember when you first said that. We were playing baseball with juvenile delinquents. You had just returned from Japan; I went to church every week just to see you.* And so on. A firetruck. And yes. Yes. It's snowing.

Man, Ladder, Wall, Elephant, and Fly

I want to know something
so fine and right I can stand in my knowing,
as I stand in a building with no walls,
but portraits hanging from them;

with no floors, but my feet
make such an ancient sound that my future
is outside each window, like people I used
to know, back to love me better.

When I say this thing I know out loud,
it will hardly sound at all.
A man on a ladder, making a wall whiter,
will think he dreamed this sound;

an elephant will think this sound
is a fly in its ear and a fly
will know this sound as something fine
and right as blood. And in my knowing,

man, ladder, wall, elephant, and fly
will all be exactly the same size, the size
of my feet or of my future, exactly the size
of the truth of this thing I know.

Cannibals

We give them sharks' eyes,
pigtails like bulls' horns
and a pursuit of autoeroticism:
no Einstein, we are sure,
could rise from a group
that scurries about on TV
like a hoard of trick-or-treaters.
And while we like our cannibals dumb
as sharks or bulls, we also need
to tame them, so TV cannibals
never rip their victims apart
to eat the heart and liver raw,
but rather simmer their victims
in large primitive pots, erstwhile
dancing like ghetto drunks
around a summer fire hydrant.

The similarity between ancient ritual
and modern religion
has been well-documented,
but I'd like to stress several points.
First, all cannibals are not the same,
any more than all existentialists
or homosexuals like the same movies
or want the same gift for Christmas.
The Efuagos of the Phillipines,
who suck the brains of their foes,
would laugh at the Dyaks of Sarawak
who eat the palms off the hands
and skin off the knees of their enemies.
Second, we are wrong to think
that cannibals are monomaniacal
about flesh—cannibals,

like everyone else, have lives
to live, jobs to do, hopes and dreams.

Take the cannibals who eat and worship trees.
It is true that each time a native dies
these cannibals eat a tourist,
but the rest of the time
this tribe does lovely things with trees.
Though eating bark does not
appeal to me, I was very moved
by the footage of an old
cannibal eating a worm.
The pulpy worm lives deep in the tree
and is considered a delicacy.
The joy with which this old cannibal
ate his worm was no different
than the delight with which we eat
raw oyster, the seriousness
with which a child in a restaurant
savors the last drop
of a watered-down Coke.

Besides, we've all tasted our own flesh.
Most of us will not admit this,
any more than we'll admit
we examine the consistency of our stool
as earnestly as we count feet in poetry.
We eat our scabs and the thin skin on blisters.
When you eat the skin around the cuticles,
you can taste your own fingerprint
in high relief—it's really
quite remarkable.

Landscape Overheard

What are men to rocks and mountains?
—Jane Austen, *Pride and Prejudice*

We're Adam and Eve camping out in paradise,
happy to live a while in parable
so long as we can bring our credit cards,
forgiving the river which shuts at dusk
now that State, not God, keeps up the land.

Though we're not the first or last to think
of escape, thus can't skinny-dip in the lake,
for fear of Girl Scouts, we're happy enough
to not ask if we're happy, almost happy
enough to stop trying not to think

of a 13th century Chinese landscape painting
we've discussed since we woke up,
far more seductive than the landscape we've got—
its drizzle of brushstrokes arbitrary
as leaves, its lonely boat grounded somewhere

in sea or air, unmoored as an idea.
We talk so much we forget to make love
and don't care, because speech is nothing more
than a hand between the thighs; words
like touches or brushstrokes are bold or delicate

and we can't help but decide to be happy,
though we know we betray the landscape
by framing it in thought as we hope for the overview
so persuasive it quiets us, makes us distant and focal
as tiny Chinese boats, centuries ago.

Exit, Pursued By a Bear

Lord, the Sunday *Times* is in!
Like children in snowsuits we go
for our papers this Saturday
night, our small fast breath
in word balloons all over
the city, before we go home
to do the crossword
in our respective beds—
can't we be friends?
You know, the smell of newsprint
in this cold makes me want
to toss a quite red tomato
into dewy greens, but mostly
this magical stage direction
from *The Winter's Tale* keeps snowing
in my head—what on earth
am I going to do with it?

Caesura

Laundry punctuates the days. Days are threaded on the wish running through them all. The wish is to never be at a laundromat alone on Christmas Eve. The laundromat is in the basement of an off-season motel, in a country where Christmas is not celebrated.

Prostitutes are suddenly dressing. They have counted the shopping days until Christmas, imagining each day as a loaded gun in a firing squad. When I see the crisp monogrammed slips that the prostitutes have, in their haste, left behind, I ask: *Why are these slips red*? The prostitutes are buying fire engines for their nephews. The prostitutes who, like me, have spoken to no one all day, not even each other, loiter at perfume displays where Russian dancers buy perfume for famous women in fur coats. The women are photographed cradling tiny bottles in their palms.

The tree outside wears its one faded star. A lost sock threads itself through the branches. I delivered a baby once on this floor. It was not an easy birth. The daughter was named Sonya, after the whore in *Crime and Punishment*.

I drink wine in the laundromat, where I am lonely. I want the prostitutes to tiptoe in on run stockings, share my wine with clean sips. I want them to stop this mannerism of shrugging their shoulders like babies wanting to be lifted up.

If most of the dancers had not defected, I would bother to learn Russian. The winter waves are a speech defect of harsh consonants.

I get my pleasure where I can.

I seem to get pleasure out of folding warm clothes.

Audience

We love a spectacle of loneliness.
The piano's stranded on the stage, the soloist
brave as Crusoe floating notes to us,
for of course the quadriplegic
lighting matches with his teeth
has no expertise until we are impressed—
how many times has he set fire to his lips
to make it look so easy now for us?
God wracked His brain inventing forests
so we could hear the lone tree falling there.

Yet in not falling, the soloist
threatens to forget his debt to us.
The weight of our attention
can't distract him long enough for one flat note,
and if it could, we might not notice,
for even this predictable sonata
has a life much greater than our concentration:
its tides reach us like a sprinkler
from a neighbor's lawn, still he plays on,
driven as the Channel swimmer—

why, it's disconcerting
that he's *happy* in his isolation tank
when only our accomplishment is having not
dozed off, not coughed or shuffled
our programs too loudly as we looked to see
if that was, indeed, Scarlatti
and if we would last until intermission
when we could go to the rest room to check
if our teeth have stained from the Burgundy,
for even we are on display;

the woman in the box across the way,
with the better view of the pianist's hands
and the *pizzicato* diamond, has more than once
provided a reminder that there is no "us":
our scores are discrete as Bach and Bartok.
I'm glad, for instance, that I'm not
that rude man clamoring from the center of a row—
he reaches the exit and keels over!
The usher shoves him through the door!
"Now it's the doctors' show," my companion warns,

to our percussive gasp, and sure enough,
the doctors' heads begin to surface
like Nessie's from her Loch, showily discreet.
Our hearts skip a beat of the encore
in wishes for the man's recovery.
The genius of merely living stays with me,
a melody quick as the ripple of foot on a pedal,
as we begin to give each other pleasure
with the dramatic development
of our virtuoso hands.

Bach

My birth was a suicide,
I was soul overboard, and what I took
for a nipple was the nose of a shark.
But you! You walk the planks

each nanosecond casual as breathing,
you kiss like a shipwrecked Greek chorus
with seaweed for lungs—I mourn your mouth!
Meanwhile, there's Bach.

At least I remember how to sublimate.
With these Two-Part Inventions
I confirm the difference
between order and repetition-compulsion.

My left hand's a flying fish,
my right hand's a swimming bird—
the hands collide on the horizon, couple,
and soar to heaven, which is underground.

See how easy to be passionate yet calm,
to drown and float at once?
You don't even have to be original:
Bach, like sex or *Lear*,

survives our infinite idiosyncrasy.
While millions may presently be playing
Number Fourteen in B Flat,
I'm willing to bet the first baby

we will never have that not one of them
is thinking about how the Inventions
are like when it first turns winter
and you can't drown the feeling

that it *has* been winter all Fall,
that soon it will be Spring;
not one is haunted by you squatting
in front of the broken TV

with your darling morbidity to whine,
"Death is the termination of all matter"—
ah, Bach! Ah, poor friend! Go
ahead, jump. Give it up. I dare you.

Present

I've longed long enough now.
Don't premeditate, surprise me with a gift!
Here's as good a time as any—

the best, in fact—to be spontaneous.
It's your only chance.
You might have done it more than once:

that July on the porch, for instance,
when you cut down the wasps' nest and said,
"I've always felt a curious affinity

with wasps"—I felt an affinity with you.
I wanted you so much
to press the nest into my hands,

kiss me in some way that meant you were there,
that even if you wouldn't be there
forever, at least you were there just then

with me, so for that moment
I could be, as I am so rarely,
just who I am and still be

all women, the only one, to whom
you are all men, the only man—
but it would have already been too late!

Each moment is eternal nympholepsy.
I want exactly what you can't give me
though I'd love to want exactly what I have—

this evening without you,
in which I am free to think of you,
to wonder, perhaps, if you're thinking of me,

so we *are* together in some sense presently,
knowing that if we were together this evening,
it would only be another one of our last.

Diner

The mind, I say, is laundry left outside to dry
for years, damp or fresh depending on an orderly
but unforeseen set of barometers. Alex
says the mind's finite, like a breadbox. Yes,
I say, like us: we'll see each other less
now that I'm in love with a man who embraces
a Random Walk theory of mind, impulses arbitrary.
Remember when Brando gets shot in *Last Tango*?
Yes, Alex says, he curls up into a fetus.
Before that, I say, he staggers onto the balcony,
so he and we get a lucid view of Paris rooftops.
Alex says the colors were rusty.
Exactly, I say: the world makes sense in just
its muddy impenetrability. That's how I feel
with Man X: I known who he is and why because
I can't. I have a poem in which a man asks,
Do you always have to rock in your chair
when you make demands? His wife retorts,
It'll be a while before you convince me
there's no difference betweem making faces
at your mother when she turns
to the oven and shoving her into it.
The poem is set in a diner, but is that enough
of an organizing principle? By next time
we speak, Man X will have left me.
Three years ago, reading *Ulysses* in Pittsburgh,
I was sure I could trace the epic
along one tendril of my asparagus fern.
Matisse, I thought, stretched the canvas
of the sky taut over Miami, where the birds
sing Wallace Stevens. Alex complains
that I've lost all but the analogic mode
of thought; he's always trying to convert

my metaphors into hypothetical statements.
My idea has always been, sit
in a polka-dotted armchair long enough,
a leather-bound Proust in your lap and your
crepe de chine soaking up a watermelon sunset,
and something is bound to happen; if not,
at least your features are reduced
to a thin, pink clarity of rhetoric, so as not
to clutter the view which is, after all, the point:
Man X's car trailing street and light, unlaced
from whatever it is that the self, in the next
line, always does like something else.
Alex says I just read too much. I say,
you should talk. I just want the self
to be found wherever we look:
at half a flag framed in the office window
at that hour too late for sleep and too early
to slip into day. I just want such facts
to resonate. You wish, Alex says.
You just want the last word.

II

Freud Is Dead

In Brooklyn a woman was sawed in half.
Half the sky went black as the headlines.
50/50 chance of falling stars: all day
we looked cautiously upwards.
The stars were lodged in our heads
like the apple in Gregor Samsa's back.
We were seeing stars.
Static from the radio cracked our walls.
Mother burned jello, her knitting needles
raged, though there was no point
in sewing any more, or buying condoms.
Poppa drank. Flatfooted Poppa,
we loved him so. Everything
made us cry. Ginger called Poppa
Do-dad and he blacked her eye.
If anyone had to urinate
they said they were freshening up.
They went as if walking on maggots.

That's not when he died.
It was much later. Years later,
maybe years before. The stars fell
elsewhere or didn't fall at all.
Our watches kept time,
skirts felt good against our legs,
our legs felt good in general.

We were happy then.
When he died
we were happy, very young,
very blond and radiant. Bells rang
unofficiously. Pearls
were found in oysters.
A light rain fell, a summer rain,
the kind you can walk home in.
A perfect rain,
as from a rain machine.

Etiquette for Automatic Writing

For my sweet sixteen
I got a chartered tour of the Aborigines.
At my banquet the guests chatted
with the classmate to their left,
no matter what. Enemies had to bury hatchets:
"I will not speak to you
because I hate your guts;
but so as not to embarrass our hostess,
please recite with me,
smiling, our multiplication tables."
All eyes watched my hand
as it fluttered down, to pick up a satin
napkin that fluttered, all fours,
to the floor.
We all wanted to elope
with the man who towed Poppa's important car.
It went dead at my party.
Ten girls in the car made towing a challenge.
We threw our hair out the window for him.
He said, "Decide among yourselves,
then write."
Thank you notes were in order, but to whom?
Aesthetic delirium set in.
I got an address from the phone directory
and wrote a nice script on a folding card:
"My next birthday is a whole year away.
What will I do in between?"
That caged grasshopper in my chest,
not the right green,
rehearsed its palpitations.

Setting the Clocks Ahead

An hour's hard to part
with as a baby tooth,
but there's freedom in rules
made to be broken.
Why mind a little jet lag
when you can leave one continent

after brunch and arrive in another
for a midnight snack the day
before, twenty-four hours younger?
Wherever you go there's bound
to be a schoolgirl in uniform:
as she bends to pull up her socks

every other second, her head
sets in a crescent against the sky
and you're blessed with a memory
of what her breasts will be—
finer than watches that work
in the grave, fine enough

to stop time, so over the planes
you can almost hear
her ovulating, the egg quick
and fatal as a dropped stitch.
Back home, your child, called in
for dinner, becomes a mother;

her child is reading next year's paper
in the nursery until all hours,
impatient for adulthood, for summer,
for a day off to reread Proust,
and the digital clock
says 3:27—my birthday!

A Maturation Poem

Childhood was small and dry as eating outside with my family in summer, flannel pajamas on, a popular tune in my head. But my parents had not mentioned orgasm. I was Ponce deLeon, Darwin. I always masturbated with the door open; I still get the safe warm feeling of rain when I hear beds creaking in adjacent apartments. Look at the clock before and after, imagine Anne Frank. Was masturbation part of her emotional experience in that slit of a house in Amsterdam? Did Helen of Troy masturbate in captivity, did Cleopatra or did she get a maidservant to do it for her, one fanning her with a feather, another tucking skinned olives into her mouth? Did Troilus ever beg Cressida to masturbate in front of him? While it's true that no one kisses like they kiss in the movies, does saying so amount to an obstinate sore-sportism, like prophesying rain all through the picnic and, when no rain comes, prophesying ants? Is there anything like an actress' nipples hardening through a satin shirt with stars stuck on it? Then her cheekbones, already dyed red from the weight of so much passion, seem to expand like Christ's hands around the last drink and fossilize, so she'll be lovely after the ball when her lips are chapped and she's coughing blood and the actor, slightly drunk, says "I can't stop looking at you," and the air around her ignites like an oven with a gas leak.

Sometimes I stare down the mirror, try to separate that face from mine. If I'm pretty I catch myself off guard like Harpo Marx with some marquise. Only when I masturbate do I totally furnish this Ellis Island called the self: then I am diagonal on the bed, with such legs as someone might desire, until I remember that legs are not the meat of great love which grows, I'm told, out of a frenzy so glaring that legs are red spots in front of the eyes, the inside of one's own retina. Know thine own self and no one who thinks kissing is silly can make you feel like an extra from *Tom Jones* being winked at across a spread of wild boar, just as you were willing to forget the wetness of your back. How will I live an enviable life in a glass house on stilts in the middle of a lake surrounded by trees with such a man?

If that is adulthood, I wish it could be a little more like boning chicken, simple and inoffensive, the perfect silky crevice between bone and skin.

The Sadness of Men

Men are born with erections and die with them.
From the first slap men stiffen and are sad.
Erections are broomsticks which propel men
from the womb and ride men into the world
so they can be Bach and the hangman, crack
the safes, make the Louisiana Purchase
and teach the dolphins to talk.

Men's lives are erections
to which each day adds a story.
We are erect, men say, and can walk away.
They invent laundry chutes
and elevators just in case,
but the most elaborate their constructions
the more confined they feel
until they get sad enough to leave
for the South Seas, the North Pole,
the jungle, the moon and, led
by the fleshy arrows that hang them each time,
start all over again, complaining over beer—
if only the beautiful women weren't so dumb,
if only the smart ones didn't talk so much!

Sad men have maps on their walls.
Sad men should get out more, have more fun.
They rock themselves to sleep at night—

> *I will build a beautiful house*
> *and dissolve myself in the house*
> *and dissolve the house*
> *in a beautiful woman's drink*
> *and live inside her forever*
> *setting off Molotov cocktails*
> *so I can be in the world again*
> *building a beautiful house.*

The Sadness of Women

Sad women trim the hedges,
dreaming of roses they'll be sent
when they suffer mastectomies.
In turnip-colored straw hats,
sadnesses strapped
like picnic tables to their backs.
The limping one is my sister.
She speaks over cluttered jets:

"This sadness is rosemilk
smeared on our skins.
A translucent Chopin sadness
at 4 AM, smoking in the kitchen
by a square red sky."

She tells me only a woman knows
the way to give blood is arbitrarily,
the way you pick a stone
to kick on the walk home.
She says, "Don't try so hard.
There will always be blood let
at the public hearings.
People will always smoke your ashes,
you can't possibly buy
enough hats to wear in their sleep.
No one will press his head
in your neck to whisper Honey,
O, lotus, babe, it's You."

The sadness of women is erudite.
It is two sad women in bunk beds
discussing the sadness.

Tornado Warning

I watch World War II on TV
with the sound off.
Across Hitler's silly, stiff salute
a tornado warning is flashed,
is threaded off screen, behind
the box, back into history.
The warning has just reached
the Führer, his mother
the servant-girl knows
he's a bad boy, it's killing her.
Soon an aeroplane will advertise
the warning in a sepia sky
above the middle ages,
where sad serfs ward off plague.
There will be no tornado.
The night is glazed and lazy.
The warning passes
without blinding me,
like a procession of cars
with lights on at noon
en route to a funeral
when no one has died,
not really.

Directions

I've tried to construct this scene like a poem.
I'm playing a mistress to someone. In his heart
is a piece of tin foil with *heart* scratched out
on it. I didn't scratch it out. He's taking me
to the country, where I'll forget to bring home
the wrapped soaps. We're stopped for gas;
he pans my leg, my awkward fingers tracing a map.

There, on the map, is a small town named Joseph.
My father's name! It's a flashback
to astronomy lessons. He let me be the moon
and circle him; I sucked in a fistful of stars
with a telescope made of his benign hands.
Limp-wristed! I shouldn't stop tracing the map,
or no one will know that I'm thinking.

I must hammer each insight into my hand.
In my picture his hand was five straws in a drink.
The hand that fed me gave me nightmares; I made him
lie down with me and cover my eyes with a cloth.
I only had eyes for him. I didn't want to bore him,
or be affected, dotting my *I*s with circles.
I'm starting small, but it's still

a half-constructed house. I'm not scared enough.
I look out the window, imagine the worst death
yet forecasted—car crash, pitiless sun,
pelvic music tinning through dismembered parts of me—
Good! Now I make it a comet of love.
I'm not only talking fear here. This is fear
of tenderness. So much we couldn't nail down.

Parting Shots

Love was an economy of gesture, a shortcut.
We curled to sleep,
lipread each other's complaints in the dark.
I saw him as a baby sees
a mobile spinning overhead.
He was porous and solid at once, like cinderblock.

I was on the porch cleaning shrimp when he left.
"It's not all black and white," he said,
but it didn't hurt. I saw right through him.
The sun set in high relief, a bullet hole
across a tidy horizontal gash.
At night there was time to contend with.

I made a list of my possessions in duplicate,
went to a movie in which children were napalmed.
My skin still tingling with guilt,
I repotted an avocado tree, thinking,
"I haven't thought about him in two hours."
An hour cut in half yielded two hours.

I pointed out to my better half
that the grass is always greener on the other side;
if it weren't one thing it would be another.
Parting my hair, I noticed that one
of my eyes is smaller than the other.
"I wonder where he went?"

Architecture

Man is no longer the master in his own house.
—Sigmund Freud

There were no good movies in town and we had to stay home, where he was "thinking" in the chair that overlooked the magnolias. I was seeing how high, and in how many configurations, I could stack our loose change, but there weren't enough pennies, so I began to make a pyramid with our soup cans. The cans made a clatter falling which distracted him. "Why don't you sit somewhere else," he suggested, "and figure out why you never went into architecture?"

The reason I am not an architect, I told him, is the movies. When I was five, one of the Three Stooges got a tooth knocked out. His grin revealed a black hole, ominous as the eye of a hurricane. I didn't want to get sucked in. Thus began my disenchantment with space. To demonstrate that the hole wasn't "real," my mother turned her back and spun around again with a black tooth. She removed a wad of black chewing gum, pressed it back on the tooth. "You see?" she said. I did. She looked like a witch. For a week I had to sleep in between my parents—I was inconsolable.

When I was sixteen, a slave in a foreign film got his arm cut off. A girl came back to school in the Fall with the stump of an arm wrapped neatly in gauze. "Bone cancer," my father said, "is very rare." She had scraped her arm in a fall and a month later it was gone. I gave up sports entirely.

My parents took my fear as emotional depth, but they were wrong. It was a discipline. I believed that if you could predict catastrophe and pay homage to it, nothing would happen. I had invented religion. Writing was my sanctuary: I locked my demons into conceptual space, where I didn't have to look at them. Revisions were Hail Marys. If I lost my arm, I could tack it back on. This worked until I ran into an insurmountable problem: if revision worked, then lightning could also strike twice in the same place; I could write off both arms and still leave arms for the world to hack. So I went into film. In film I got flesh—the real stuff— but it was flat and distant, a layer of light, less substantial than ink. I could go backstage and put my demons' makeup on, dress them up as saints. "Why fool with boards and nails," I concluded, "when the house of fantasy is indestructable?"

He looked at me coldly. "The process of increasing mental strength you have described," he said, "is called growing up. It has little to do with film and fiction or fact and fantasy; it has virtually nothing to do with architecture. You went into film because you can't add."

I stacked my coins viciously until I thought of a retort. "The real reason I am not an architect," I told him, "is you. You are taxing. You are dense. I spend all my time smuggling ideas through to you. I could have been anything. I could have been an archaeologist; I could have been a taxidermist or—"

"—or a pair of claws scuttling across the ocean floor. Did film teach you evasion? Get to the point."

I told him he'd cut off my options. I told him to go back to his wife.

"You think I'm going to leave," he said. "If I accept your theory, you're sending me away in the hope of keeping me here."

One of my penny stacks fell. I couldn't decide if that was approval or censure of my new theory. The other stacks stayed put, negating the Domino Theory.

"Hold me," I said.

Chiasma

Like the lost glove behind the radiator
or the suicide note in invisible ink
under the warp in the floorboard,
the secret place is there all along
only hidden, because the world
is a blind spot, and even what's ahead
is dimmed by the windshield.
No vehicle, however space-aged,

will get you there; no divining rod
can locate the entrance
like a diamond in continents of sand;
to be systematic, in fact, is anathema
to magic, which, like Newton's apple,
is always accidental,
the birth certificate of a rabbit
in the lining of a hat so tattered

you give it to Goodwill,
where a virgin buys it to contain
the unicorn plant that keeps growing
after her solitary death.
The world's in a teacup
you remove to dust the cabinet—
you hum something ordinary
your grandmother used while bathing you,

or maybe you heard it on the radio
just yesterday while trying to remember
what you'd forgotten at the store,
and there it is, sharp as a postcard,
especially if found in sleep
where the clearest images emerge
like holograms of elves—
like cellar monsters too, it's true,

for there's no Eden without its snake,
no Oz without its wicked witch,
no sex without the threat of syphilis.
The sexual nature of the secret place
is, of course, explicit:
the slit from which you enter it
is tight as the Bermuda Triangle
of a young girl's genitals

and the place is safe as womb
until penetrated by the noise and dirt
that pollute the best neighborhoods
after Original Sin—
the irritation that, though unpleasant
for the oyster, makes the pearl.
It shouldn't surprise us that sex,
so joyous and terrifying at once,

can only be discussed topologically.
All beliefs have their superego, ego and id,
their heaven, earth and hell,
because this is the only world we know.
The world's inspired; we breathe it,
literally, as a plant breathes sun,
as a woman flowers to inhale a man.
You survey the place—a little like Bolivia,

you think, or New Zealand, though it's neither—
from the warmth of a fjord.
The insects on the foliage,
even from this height, are in a high relief
magnified by the exotic silence—
no church bells, no bells on the grazing cows,
no life more demanding than the moss
on the sides of buildings that are curiously

modern, given their antiquity.
It's quiet and there's no one.
No one, at least until you make the ancient
mistake of thinking that a secret,
like a buried treasure or an unsung aria,
is useless until admired.
Soon the place is overrun with tourists—
if, that is, you can find it again;

betrayed, such places usually vanish.
The loss is worse than a moth hole
in a favorite sweater or the last eyedrop
from the Fountain of Youth
coughed into the ocean.
You suspect you'll never feel a pain
or happiness that pure again, although
just now, outside the window

where the dusk's unseasonably bright,
a dog lifts his leg against
a strange parallelogram of light.
Following the arc the dog makes,
you reach a single daisy
growing at the foot of the mailbox.
If you stare at the center of the daisy
and nothing happens, at least you're not much older.

Make-Up

The mask is the face.
    —Jean Cocteau

For a while we liked the truth.
We'd learned that sugar lobotomizes,
that our leaders are thugs
and if we tried to punish them
they'd only play ping-pong in prison
with executioners paid out of our pockets
as other men went to the moon through
an ozone already poisoned by our deodorants.
If there was napalm in our water,
if our birthday cakes gave our unborn cancer
and even the ground beneath us
shifted over Love Canals,
we had a right to know—

how adorably *Christian* we still were!
Our horror films all featured devils.
There was evil everywhere, but God
helps those who help themselves
and admire His work:
we grew vegetables outside simple houses
and canceled trivial differences
in earthly position imposed
by racism, sexism and I.Q. testing
with a denim unpretentious
as Mao suit or nun's habit,
confident that we'd never be deceived
by a gargoyle in a nice tuxedo.

But even then, the truth was never plain.
Though seeing is believing,
certain chemicals ratified by nature
could expand or tune the focus on the realm
of the visible; our guitars were attached
to amplifiers, and if we eschewed
the technology of neutron bomb,
electric chair and pocket calculator,
our bodies were our finest instruments:
jogging, vitamins and Yoga made us limber
so we could vary the missionary position
as often as possible with as many partners
as could make us too sublimely tired

for the workaday world.
If the technology of our sex lives
was only a different kind of assembly line,
planned obsolescence and conspicuous
consumption, what of it?
There was always The Song of Songs
to justify our hedonism as a component
of our righteousness, and besides
as instruments in God's symphony
we were different drummers—
though science was kind of establishment,
at least The Heisenberg Uncertainty Principle
had proven Subjective Relativism!

While there's a contradiction
between saying what's heaven for the goose
is hell for the gander and insisting
that anyone who wears a bra
or prefers Sinatra to the Beatles
should be shot at dawn if only
we didn't know beyond a shadow
of a doubt that capital punishment is wrong,
if we contradicted ourselves,
well then we contradicted ourselves—
every ideology is circular,
every believer closed to reason,
and it was part and parcel of our charm

to be something new yet tied
to the best traditions East and West,
spiritual and political.
If we were going mad—and madness
was a national sport, second only to sex—
it was because we saw too much,
because we'd closed ourselves off
only to closing ourselves off,
knew that there was nothing unequivocally ugly
just as there was nothing purely good.
Abraham Lincoln, we'd found out,
was a manic-depressive; George Washington
may have destroyed a *forest* of cherry trees;

Louisa Mae Alcott and Horatio Alger
both wrote pornography on the sly;
and though we were impressive on D-Day,
we entered the war too late
for all of the wrong reasons,
not to mention killing all those Japanese
people in their sleep like bullies.
Why shouldn't we be mad?
We'd be mad not to be, we agreed, and went
to movies in which the mad were the only
people in their right minds,
winning single-handed against the system—
of course the mad were good-looking
and strong, for we were still Americans,

and could no more surrender the notion
that a good man had white teeth
and Olympic biceps, even while our men
had long hair and our women unshaved
underarms, than we could believe
the Japanese made better cars than we,
the Swiss better clocks, the Russians
better spaceships or the French
better love—our modesty,
our honesty were ours alone;
we were the best expatriots;
certainly in *admitting* failure
we had triumphed prettily.

Concurrently, of course, the question
of nature and nurture was reintroduced
when science suggested once again
that madness was nothing more
than a chemical imbalance readily cured
by drugs which, though not yet
perfected, might eventually eliminate
the need for all that tiresome,
old-fashioned soul-searching.
If we contended that too many
nitrites in our frozen food
would make us stupid, television
and ghetto life make us assassins—

that the world made us and we,
by remaking our world, could make ourselves—
then what would we do if it turned out
that beauty, brains and brawn
were God-given gifts all along,
that madness and death were programmed
at birth, that despite flunking school
Einstein and Edison were *meant*
to be geniuses as surely as Hitler
would have been a bastard
even given the best liberal arts education?
If there was no chicken, in short,
then where did all those eggs come from?

The chicken on one hand, the egg on the other
each had a half dozen in its favor:
our forefathers were convinced that all men
are created equal, that man is born free
and everywhere he is in chains,
but our forefathers were also Calvinists
who believed in Manifest Destiny
and certainly we wouldn't like to deny
the supremacy of individuality—
left to the Indians, America
would have never made New York, where one
can be a poet and not starve to death
or be laughed off the face of the earth.

Boy were we confused—still are!
For all those years we were split.
We had all the facts, but couldn't fit
them together; we were like the paranoid
schizophrenic who's not only right,
but extraordinarily perceptive
on the particulars—i.e.
his wife went for a walk
at exactly ten AM and smiled
at the postman just as it began to rain,
giving him a headache; and dead wrong
on the conclusion—i.e., his wife
is unfaithful and he's Napoleon.

Meanwhile, it's several decades later
and time for dinner;
the economy's such a wreck
that we can't afford veal,
which is what we feel like eating,
and even if veal fell from the sky,
removing our anachronistic guilt
about butchering baby cows,
we don't know anymore
who's supposed to cook dinner, now
that Mom's a soldier, Dad a seamstress
and all the children we're having fewer of
going into business administration,

completing the all-too-common full-circle
which history has repeated
often enough for us to predict
that the atheist's child will be a preacher,
the socialist's child a Republican.
Is it any wonder that we want
to recuperate inside for a while
with a candle lit, a centerpiece
of fresh flowers, matching china,
good wine, a gourmet dinner
and the unalienable right to the pleasure
of our own good looks?
We're allowed to *dress up* again!

We're even allowed to put on make-up
and improve upon what nature gave us—
it's not just a privelege to do so,
but a responsibility, our social conscience
bidding us once more to do our best.
Besides, we were never meant to think
that these wings of blue and pink,
this shine on a woman's face is "real,"
any more than we believe the Empress'
bound feet grew that way, the actress
really cries on stage or the villain
in the play is really dead
when he falls over so convincingly.

Just as we've begun to miss
the suspension of disbelief in art,
to wish that the characters
would find their author already,
that the author would oblige us
with an illusion of depth
by making the characters likable
with problems we can care about
and see resolved, so too
have we begun to crave friends and lovers
who we find pleasant and kind
as well as "interesting"—
we want to have a good time again

like kids in the first snow of winter
on Christmas day, and when our dogs die
or we get fired or are simply
out-of-sorts with the weather and middle age,
it would be nice to have someone say
"I'm sorry" without irony
so we can believe that our presence
makes some difference even if
we haven't made a million dollars,
written a best-seller, had a baby
and a breakdown or provided
some brilliant comments on how
castration anxiety is dating as a theory.

In all those years of turning molehills
into mountains, we have only made
of our inability to "relax"
another epiphanic failure and subject
for a self-help book—it tries the patience.
If I say "I like your dress" and you say
"This old thing?" why have we been
more beholden to hollow convention
than if we compare writers' blocks or orgasms?
Anyway, what's wrong with the comfort
of convention? If I manage to be fun
all evening then thank you for dinner,
am I necessarily shallow or a liar?

With cosmetics you can make a hook nose
smaller, small eyes bigger, the cheekbones
more pronounced, the lashes thicker,
the lips moister and the eyebrows
more of a perfect half-circle,
creating at least from a distance
a temporary confidence that the face
is not an affront to the cultural ideal—
I personally look forward
to the return of paleness and obesity
as desirable qualities, but until then
a made-up face is nice as waxed floors,
a wrapped gift, or a trimmed lawn,

and I intend to convince as many
onlookers as possible that even if behind
this aging flesh there's slag and banality,
the skin at least is not offensive,
nor are the manicured nails and the wardrobe,
planned for variation in color and texture
and for doing to the body what make-up
does to the face, like if you're short-waisted,
your belt should match your pants,
if long-waisted, your shirt;
like yellow and red look terrible
on fair skin, brown and mauve
unbecoming on the olive-complexioned.

That our fashions will soon be obsolete
as bustles or powdered wigs
doesn't trouble me—by then
I'll be too old to look good anyway,
and will hopefully be able to rest
on whatever laurels I've accumulated
by virtue of hard work and experience.
Besides, thinking about the appearance
not only kills some time, but provides
a useful model of what it would be like
to lift the face of the entire planet,
and presently, alas, we must
be content to start small.

Skinner Remembers a Fall

Why do women wear those shoes?
She was, for the moment she slipped,
a pedestrian beating the light.
Only that. I stopped to help;
she caught sight of me as her papers flew,
seemed to know me, as one knows
a dog the same breed as one's own—
perhaps another white-haired man
once helped her, in a similar circumstance.

Someone pointed, said, "That's Skinner"—
the name clinical, a large corporation.
I remembered a side-street in Georgetown,
stopping my limousine as a woman
exited her house, tripped and fell.
Everything was white—house, dress,
shoes, hat; the blood
stood out, startling
as the drips in a Pollock.

I saw the falling girl again that night
in a small café, defending graphology.
"Handwriting analysis," she said,
"is my religion. Processes are reduced
to a dance of energy, a choreography
of cause. The hand that moves the pen
shapes the character, is shaped by it;
God is the hand that moves the world."
The pretty high-heeled girl didn't know me.

I'd helped her up; now she was eating.
I had nothing to say to her.
I thought: I am B.F. Skinner,
this is Manhattan, Thursday,
and *I* should thank *her*:
things are as they should be,
just as they seem, pure transparency:
painful, joyous, like air
at high altitudes.

III

Mind the Quiet

Couldn't say
a word if the sky weren't so quiet,
mighn't even mind
the quiet if the color of the sky
weren't the fragile pink
of a pill at the back of my throat.
Believe me, I'd rather not

talk, but the street
is more hushed than an old poem,
children play in the parking lot
like slow Chinese characters that mean
embarrassment of riches—
if I don't say something now
the children will grow up too

fast, find themselves elegantly
dressed in Paris, trying
too hard to have a good time,
voices like spring water intoning
There's only one bird left in America
and it's just about to be shot
from a highway with a quiet gun.

Thank You, Leo Tolstoi, Thanks

The ragged seraphim are scavenging
again behind the mortuary
with ragged roses in hair and teeth
and I am a bird of paradise
though not in Russia or a Countess

I want a dozen children by Monday
to send in bloomers to play
behind the mortuary
to tell every passerby
I had lived quite unconsciously

and felt quite outside
the conditions of normal
existence until I met you
O you there you with the mouth or
you O someone

April Fool's Day

Love is not in season and friends
are an endangered species. We have chosen
the zoo as one of those rare glib feats
of order—green on St. Patrick's—
and though grief is the dominant gene
we like this much: it is the zoo.
The sky is opaque as Pernod.
A lawnmower goes somewhere;
I am here with her
through some prank of natural selection.

People come in twos. One couple
holds a hand mirror up to the monkeys,
who look past their mirrored faces
for the rest of the monkey
as I look past the day
at the zoo, which is the poem, by saying:
That tall man sketching on a bench
by the flamingos, is he watching us?
The woman who is my friend
moves hair from her eyes, and I

want to do it for her, the way monkeys
part each other's fur to find lice.
Wouldn't you love, she asks, *to be*
an animal, to be that free?
I tell her no, I wouldn't sacrifice
the right to smoke or sketch on a bench,
longing to be an animal.
The sentence passes
like children at a zoo, chasing peacocks
behind the trees where the sun has gone;

the pavement is off-color
after the pink, disfigured shine
of an Orangutan's ass.
I miss the poem I haven't yet written
and the day, which already feels, by five,
like a childhood memory of zoos.
I will remember knowing I'd remember
wanting to stroke the cagey sun,
shelve the light more evenly
on the horizon,

like the lines of a poem that is a resumé
of days spent at zoos,
those heirlooms.

No More Poems

Let us have no more poems like Japanese trick boxes, I said, no more four-leaf clover keychain poems, no pasteurized poems, I said. Too many poets spoil this party. We're all magicians performing for magicians; let's make a pact to keep our rabbits in our hats! Some discussion, but I made no friends. Got in late, dreamed my mother died, woke up at dawn so shaken I had to call her then walk around in my neighborhood, reminding myself I love my mother, I love my street, I love the Keats line "Thank you for the lovely dish of filberts." The pianos were gorgeous in the shop windows.

Teaching Him to Read

As always, the first question is why.
When it doesn't look like rain
he drives with the top down;
one flash of his hand on the stick shift
and women recross their legs—believe me,
making love with him is like singing Giovanni
straight through on one lungful of sunlight
before the greatest maestro in the history
of Europe, on the first summer
day in Siberia after a century
of solitary confinement, so in a sense
he already knows the classics.

I can't tempt him with last wills or maps
to the treasure—money doesn't interest him
more than the taste of veal
pounded thin as the brows of his women.
I can't tempt him with vicarious pleasure—
he's too happy to crave battles, intrigues,
caviar on yachts; nor can I tempt him
with his armchair on a rainy night,
for without a woman he'd enjoy
the rain itself, his solitude.
I can't threaten him with reveries
of educated men—he gets their women;

I can't tease him with the fun he'd have
reading praise for him in ladies' diaries—
he isn't vain. So why should he read?
I tell him I don't know. Do it for me.
So in bed we begin with an anatomical alphabet
(ass, breast, cuticle, etc.) and over dinner
we do food; by dessert he has mastered place
enough to recite a litany of women
from an Alice in Alabama to a Zanzibar Zazu
he never told me about, and soon we're ready
for the heart—its anxieties, befuddlements,
consternations and delights.

Heart and mind take him a week.
He knows harder, faster, more and now,
but many feelings (like defensiveness)
are new to him, so I must demonstrate,
and we come close to a tiff when I express
impatience: until now he has ordered
in restaurants by soliciting recommendations,
but now he insists on reciting the entire menu
and having it explained, which is irritating
when you're hungry and the menu's in Chinese.
I've been wrong to move him too quickly
to nouns like despair and projection

before fully acquainting him with the written
language—he must learn to print.
We go back to basics, again in bed.
I urge him to trace a D with a blunt pencil
on my lifted knee, an S on the sinuousness
of my inner ear and so forth, until
he can link the shapes of the letters
with simple forms found in nature.
Soon he's ready to print on my body
with his tongue, providing some distraction
for me and a valuable review
of the vowels embedded in my pleasure for him.

He has seen no other women.
I've been demanding as a football coach,
while he has become so devoted to his study
that he leaves notes on his car—"Out To Lunch,"
"Gone Fishing"—and revels in the obvious
ironies. So far at least, I don't miss
my wild child. He is neither wild nor child,
and at this point in his life, language
will only rarefy his consciousness.
Now there's the problem of selecting texts.
He isn't confident enough for too many
words like vituperative—I myself get frustrated

when I have to look up more than five
words per page; but the simply written books
are mostly pornography, fables and war stories,
which I deem unsuitable, so an initial
selection includes the Bible, the newspaper
and several Dick and Jane readers
which may provide a lighthearted
introduction to sociology.
Needless to say, he owns none of these texts.
We haven't been apart for a moment in two months,
but I'm afraid a library or newsstand
may overwhelm him, so I leave him at home

and head out into April's articulate silence.
When I return, he's in bed with a petite
Japanese girl who speaks no English—
he's teaching her bed, window, shadow, door.
My jealousy would senselessly bar
his progress: I understand the male passion
for dominance and besides, it's healthy for him
to get a sense of how far he has come,
so I bow low as a geisha and leave him
to his play. After a while I bring the paper
and suggest he fill his girlfriend in on world
events; he consents and even invites me

to join them as they read aloud.
I couldn't be prouder if my own child
who two months ago was still playing house
were suddenly to play Lizst to a standing
room only crowd in Paris—speaking of my child,
I'm sure she's beginning to wonder where I am,
as will be my husband, if he's done
campaigning yet (he's a politician;
in fact, he's on the front page,
and we discuss his policies naked on sheets
printed with cherries). I vow to return as soon
as I'm sure my student will continue productively.

I have the teacher's joy in experiencing
the world anew through my pupil's eyes
as we read marquees, headlines, the Song of Songs.
Our delicious sensory overload is threatened
when my husband's detective confronts me
in a ladies' bathroom and demands that I return
to speechwriting for the sake of my husband's
career, but I trade her a night with my student
for several more weeks to get the language
under his belt, as there are still some kinks
in his comprehension—most notably, he does not
yet have a selective attention.

He reads the sign for the Bureau of Abandoned
Vehicles with the same earnestness
he turns towards *The Tale of Genji*.
His lack of discrimination is, of course,
part of his charm: it's why he loves my ear
as much as other openings, why
he loves other women as much as me,
why I could interest him in reading to begin with;
but I want him to understand tone, structure,
syntax, theme, alliteration, and he still
has trouble with puns—when,
in one of my husband's speeches

(I'm writing them again, mailing them
from a fictitious return address) I type drowning
for crowning glory, my pupil doesn't even laugh.
His reading, in short, is not sensitive.
He might as well be eating hotcakes, me,
or one of the countless other women, younger than I,
who continually interrupt our sessions. Still,
these have been the finest years of my life:
when I look up from "Byzantium" to the TV
which he has switched on, my life with him seems
like a surprise nap that continued past dinner.
On the TV my daughter's twelve, my husband Senator!

Both my lover and I are considerably older.
To allay the shock I ask to make love;
he discovers a lump in my breast and moments later
I'm drugged for a mastectomy. The last thing
I remember before going under is him ogling
the nurse at the foot of my bed, a pile of books
slipping from his lap to the floor,
or did I imagine that? And did I dream
my daughter with nipples packed as microfilm
standing still for his inspection?
Why are the nursès lined up like that in their white,
angelic as blank pages, beaming at him?

I wake up later without breasts, without husband,
daughter, lover, or student—a man who'd ravage
Anne Frank, Helen Keller I was bound to lose.
Cancer spreads, but loving him is like trying
to start a fire in the rain
with books that had long ago sprouted lichen.
Before we've even had time to consider
the commonplace nature of our plot, he's gone.
A nun by my bedside is smiling and bobbing
as if nothing has happened,
and in a sense, in an oddly literary
sense, dear lord, nothing has.

The Madonna Has That Look Again

As if she just remembered
that the child isn't hers, after all—
she'd hoped for a simpler life.

The Wise Men are there, of course:
uncles whose jokes aren't funny,
whom one must invite. Even they

aren't right. There's too much age
in their smiles, already etched
deep as cracks in canvas. The child

sees himself in another distance.
Despite the baby fat, his face,
against her robe, already fades,

is already the Holy Shroud of Turin,
as if he knows how hard it is
to pose for a family portrait—

they've sat too long already
for spontanaiety. The Madonna's lap
is already petrified; the child

is far from her as he will be
looking down, from the cross,
at the parquet floor of the museum.

God's Jukebox

God's tunes are so firm you want to sleep on them
to dream ambitious colors atonal as snow in July
or a sonnet entitled "Sisyphus with Chickenpox"
in which you light the wrong end of your cigarette
again but the orgying angels sigh and applaud.
God's saxophone knows the sweet deep truth
of your mother coming the night she conceived you,
and once you hear God's tunes you can't get them
out of your head though you can't remember them.
Even if you don't believe in him—maybe especially
if you'd rather believe in your pet or *savoir-faire*—
your head's lit up like God's pinball machine
and, all silly in your Sunday best,
you're the most serious tone God ever punched.

Without a God

Genius is easy: invent the sandwich and there's no stopping us; we go out at strange hours in our orange cape and hip boots, proud that we and no other animal thought of using music for purposes other than mating. At least we've earned the right to be bored enough to plant dynamite in each other's birthday cakes, or to go a whole day without saying the word *I*, the word *the*, the word *like*. But without a god it is harder to be competent. It is when we're cooking for eight on a shoestring and out of butter. When other people win a week for two in Switzerland for the best explication of our text, and when we finally notice that everyone else in the world can run to answer the phone without panting. Then we need a god to remind us that crushing the spider on a pillow is a moral decision, that millions of neurons must reach an agreement before we can bend in our chairs to pick up our pencils, no less hone razors that miraculously disappear in our worst enemies' apples.

Without a god we can't sit for a minute in the center of the floor with our fists in our eyes, whining that we want ice cream, that we want the ice cream man with the muscles to come right now, knowing that God will punish us for such gutlessness, that if only we would get up at once and sweep the floor and get on with it, the ice cream man would come in a bomb of light, wearing all of our favorite colors, and singing our national anthem so loud that it's best to ignore him, rubbing up to each other by accident, and smearing ice cream on each other's lips as if there were no tomorrow.

If You Could See This

If you could see this under glass,
against a white wall,
it would look quite different;
first of all sometimes there are no
seats, and people have to stand
near the fountain, where the plants
contradict everything that mothers
say about the effect of mirrors
in a small space; furthermore
people insist on letting you know
what they abhor, so a glare
complicates the colors, which would be
okay on their own, if they'd stop
blushing under their own weight
and calling themselves names
in the hope that you'll forget to;
and why do people always stare at you
when you are faking concentration,
so you want not to sit there
anymore, looking at the nudes;
you would rather examine the hairs
bristling your thighs in the chrome
of the washroom, not that you harbor
any affection for the washroom,
but simply because your shoes,
against the tiles, seem to grow away
from you and flatten
into something microscopic,
something you would like
to stand back and examine
under glass, against a white wall.

Because I Can't

The heat tonight is a bad argument
I can't refute.
My talk is vaporous—more humidity.

I want talk to curve
like the small of your back,
a line which redefines,

if only for a match flame's time,
the shape of my thinking.
I talk to make of the night and us

a certainty I can't refute.
I talk because I can't
knead your skull hard or precisely

enough to read the Braille
of your thought; because
your skull seems so small sometimes,

so frail and definite,
that I know I can hold you
no more than I can hold my future,

though your back,
as you turn, is nebulous
and sound as sleep.

Dolphins Can't

Sleep's the head of a baby
born while someone yawns
in the three blue minutes
earlier it got dark tonight.
Don't clutch sleep's twitches,

even with fingers gauzed
by shadows from leaves.
Admit no poets or aunts to coo
by sleep's crib in the library,
turn away the boarder

with the rubber shoes and violin,
don't even trust the curtains,
behind them too many crickets
threaten to kidnap the dust
off sleep's birth certificate.

If it weren't for the snow
that gestates to fall three months
from now, we could hear sleep talk
its baby talk, more essense than sense.
Dogs can't hear it, dolphins can't.

Sleep's speech is so tiny and slow
it's more like a texture—
pubic hair growing under the skin,
baby's breath taking in sun
on a heath in Ireland.

A Facsimile of the Rosetta Stone

The museum, I was told, held two lovers
who died over a thousand years ago
during a volcanic eruption,
preserved in an unguarded moment
of passion, the woman's hand
actually clutching the man's face.

Stupidly, I expected to see skin.
These skeletons were sexless,
faceless, grinning as skulls grin—
no noise, no hair, no shiny tongues.
You could tell from their positions
in the glass coffin that they hadn't

died during the act, but afterwards:
she curls towards him to tease his face;
he's on his back with hand on hip
as if to say, I refuse to work today,
I won't even call in sick, let's
just keep screwing—if, in fact,

they were lovers at all:
he was twenty, she twenty-two;
if clothed they might seem siblings,
neighbors, friends from school.
Furthermore, no volcano killed them;
they were in a bin hiding from a war,

apparently not hiding very well,
for his skull's bashed, her ribcage crushed.
Their casual pose is more heroic
in response to a war than to a volcano;
still, I wanted them to die surprised,
in love, and from their bones

you can't even tell if the blows
interrupted them in act or sentence,
if they suffocated in their sleep
and were killed later as an afterthought,
or maybe they were damaged in transport
to the museum—I was disappointed.

Next we saw the mummies.
With all the glass and swaddling
you can't see much but several decayed
fingers; even the mural on the backdrop
of red and gold kings and queens
in their obscene contortions seems quite lively

next to the mummies—how did they expect
to have fun in death, bound up like that?
My friend wanted to talk Egyptology
until she got distracted
by the Rosetta Stone, which was supposed
to be in London, but there it was,

unguarded, on a wall beside a case
of boring ancient vases in Philadelphia.
Just as you could tell the male skeleton
from the female skeleton by their gestures,
you could tell that only politicians
would go on and on in such

a claustrophobic hand, that what they said
is not important, merely bureaucratic;
what matters is not needing
to know what's said to understand,
like when you overhear a lovers'
quarrel in a restaurant

in a foreign language and know all
you care to know about the strangers' lives.
Still, I wanted to be more excited.
I knew that if I knew more
I would not assume I understood
the Stone; if I had been the archaeologist

who deciphered it I'd be more moved
by the mute impassivity of stone;
the words would blur like the face
of a lover you know too well, until
even in the act of love—no,
especially in the act—you can't recall

this stranger's face, these hieroglyphic
gestures, and the act itself
is something that might
have happened to you years ago.
You may even find yourself
thinking of something else entirely,

like the Rosetta Stone or how
you'd like to die
alone on a porch after love,
right when the sky darkens before
a storm on an August evening.
Then you're surprised by your own

pleasure, as you're surprised
when you're explaining something important
to a lover who indicates with a gesture
that lovemaking is more important then,
or as my friend was surprised
to mention something about the Stone

and find me inattentive, thinking
about love and poems on love,
thinking that if she were a lover and not
a friend, we could make love right here
on the floor of the museum
and really understand the Rosetta Stone.

She ran a finger across the Stone—
a lover's gesture, as if stone were thigh.
I don't know why, but I slapped her hand.
The gesture made us laugh, but the truth
is I was petrified: Lord, I thought,
please don't ever send a bomb off

and make me die not writing,
not making love or saving the Rosetta Stone,
but slapping the hand of a friend
in a Philadelphia museum and laughing,
petrified, at two in the afternoon
on Thursday, January tenth, nineteen eighty.

Mime Flautist

When they ask for my last wish
I tell them to find the mime flautist.
There is only one mime flautist
with hands like time-lapsed flowers
who played outside my open window
in the middle of summer, of night,
before the third world war, before
mankind got its sixth finger back.
He played the same song
he always plays, a song older
than Mozart or dinosaurs
which I never heard but knew,
read off his lips and fingers.
As he played I thought of the day
I wore a white jacket
I hadn't worn in years, and found
in the left-hand pocket
where I never put things a handkerchief
which I knew was the handkerchief
I cried on at my father's funeral,
which my mother cried on
at her father's funeral,
which her father cried on the day
he lost the rocking horse
with one eye, a century ago.
Though I am blindfolded
when the mime flautist arrives,
I know he is there,
for I am about to say something
I'd give my life to say,
one word older than the handkerchief
which blindfolds me, even older
than the flautist's song,

one word I'll be shot as I utter,
a word like linen
someone will find years from now
and know exactly when
I said it, exactly
why.